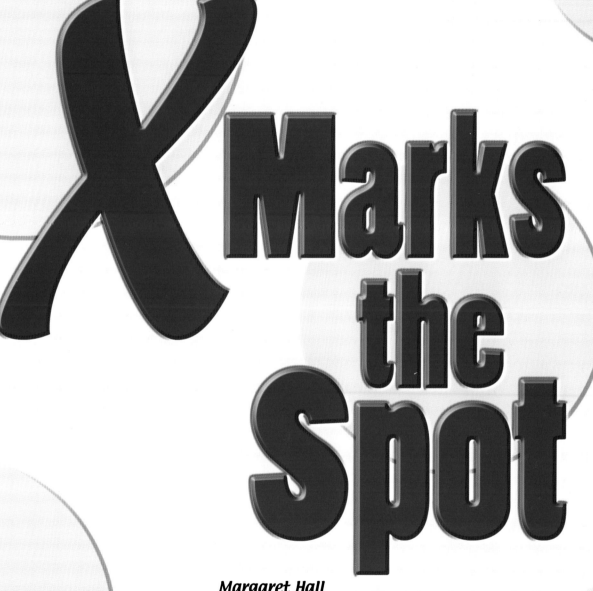

X Marks the Spot

Margaret Hall

Raintree

Chicago, Illinois

© 2007 Raintree
Published by Raintree,
A division of Reed Elsevier Inc.
Chicago, Illinois

Customer Service 888-363-4266

Visit our website at www.heinemannraintree.com

Designed by Michelle Lisseter and Bigtop
Printed and bound in China by WKT

11 10 09 08 07
10 9 8 7 6 5 4 3 2 1

**Library of Congress
Cataloging-in-Publication Data**
Hall, Margaret, 1947-
  X marks the spot / Margaret Hall.
    p. cm.
  Includes bibliographical references and index.
  ISBN 1-4109-2600-1 (lib. bdg. : hardcover) -- ISBN 1-4109-2629-X (pbk.)
  1. Cartography--Juvenile literature. I. Title.
  GA105.6.H35 2006
  526.09--dc22
                                        2006008783

13 digit ISBNs
978-1-4109-2600-5 (hardcover)
978-1-4109-2629-6 (paperback)

Acknowledgments
The author and publisher are grateful to the following for permission to reproduce copyright material: Alamy/Robert Harding Picture Library Ltd. **p. 11**; Ancient Art & Architecture/R. Sheridan **p. 16**; The Art Archive/Bibliothèque des Arts Décoratifs Paris/Dagli Orti **p. 21**; The Art Archive/Bodleian Library Oxford **pp. 8, 13**; The Art Archive/Musée Lapérouse Albi/Dagli Orti **p. 18**; Bridgeman Art Library/British Museum **p. 7** (bottom); Corbis **p. 10** (Michael Freeman); Corbis/Bettmann **p. 23**; Getty Images **p. 26**; Getty Images/PhotoDisc **p. 9**; Harcourt Education Limited/Tudor Photography **p. 27**; NASA **p. 25**; National Maritime Museum, London **p. 19**; New York Subway **p. 4**; Science Photo Library/Library of Congress **p. 15**; Unknown **pp. 7** (top), **28**.

Cover photograph of a 17th century illustrated map of the Americas and navigation instrument reproduced with permission of Getty Images/Stone/Sean Ellis.
Picture research by Mica Brancic and Maria Johannou.

Illustrations by Darren Lingard.

The publishers would like to thank Nancy Harris and Daniel Block for their assistance in the preparation of this book.

Every effort has been made to contact copyright holders of any material reproduced in this book. Any omissions will be rectified in subsequent printings if notice is given to the publishers.

Contents

What Is a Map?   4

The First Maps   6

Maps for Travelers   8

Charting the Coasts   12

Changing Views of the World   14

New Mapmaking Tools   18

Up in the Air   20

High-Tech Mapping   22

Then and Now   28

Glossary   30

Want to Know More?   31

Index   32

Some words are printed in bold, **like this**. You can find out what they mean on page 30. You can also look in the box at the bottom of the page where they first appear.

What Is a Map?

How can you find your way around a new place? You can use a map! A map can show the whole world. Or it can show a small part of the world, such as a town.

Some maps tell you about the land. They show lakes and rivers. They also show islands and mountains. Other maps show roads and cities. They show **borders** between countries or states. Borders are imaginary lines. These lines separate different places.

Some maps show ▶ *small areas. This map shows a city's subway system. A subway is an underground travel system.*

Mapmakers are called **cartographers**. They make maps for different reasons. Road maps help take travelers where they want to go. There are maps of neighborhoods and parks. There are even maps of the ocean floor!

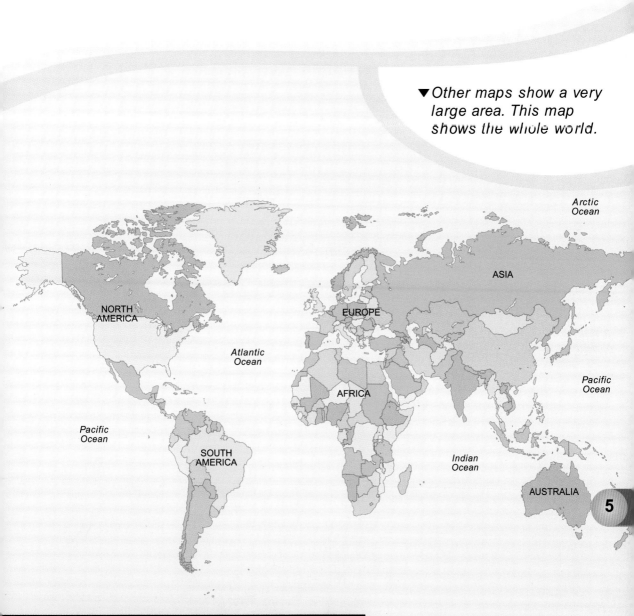

▼ *Other maps show a very large area. This map shows the whole world.*

border	imaginary line that separates land
cartographer	person who makes maps

5

The First Maps

Long ago, the Greeks, Chinese, and Arabs were the best mapmakers. They knew a lot about the world. But their maps did not show all of Earth. That is because they only knew about part of the world. They only knew about the places that people around them had seen.

Ptolemy was a Greek **cartographer**. A cartographer is a mapmaker. Ptolemy lived in Egypt. He was the first to put north at the top of a map. He also had a new idea. The idea was to make maps of small parts of the world. These maps could show more about a place.

Ptolemy put his maps in a book. His book was kept in a library. For about 200 years, people visited the library. They used Ptolemy's maps. Then the maps were lost.

Hand drawn

Long ago, maps were all drawn by hand. They cost a lot of money. Few people could afford to buy maps.

6

TIMELINE

| 500 BC | 400 BC | 300 BC | 200 BC | 100 BC | 0 |

▼ *This map of the world was drawn in 1520. It uses Ptolemy's ideas.*

◀ *This clay map is thousands of years old. The mapmaker thought the world was a flat disk.*

AD 150

Ptolemy finishes his book of maps.

AD 391

Ptolemy's maps are lost.

AD 100   AD 200   AD 300   AD 400   AD 500   AD 600

Maps for Travelers

Travelers told people about the places they saw. They talked about how they got to these places. **Cartographers** talked to travelers. They used what they learned to make better maps.

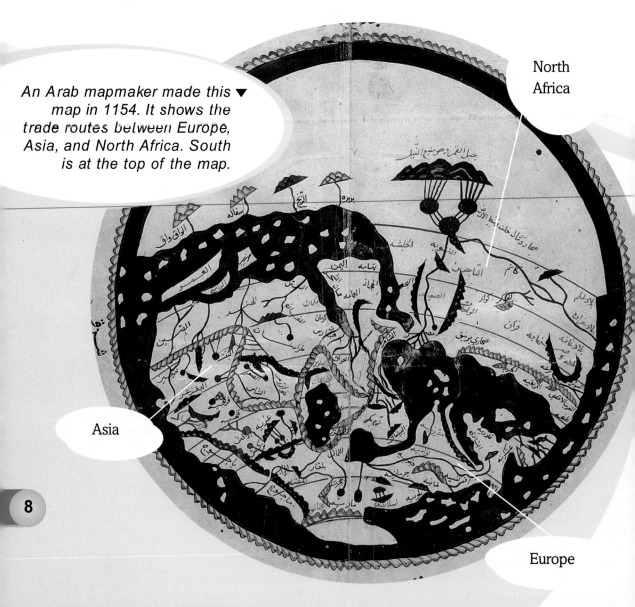

An Arab mapmaker made this ▼ map in 1154. It shows the trade routes between Europe, Asia, and North Africa. South is at the top of the map.

North Africa

Asia

Europe

compass tool that tells directions

Maps helped traders. But it was still hard for traders to find their way. They used tools that depended on the Sun. But the tools did not work on cloudy days.

A new invention made it easier to use maps. This invention was the **compass**. A compass has a needle that moves. The ends always point to spots near Earth's North Pole and South Pole. Now travelers knew where north was. This helped them use their maps. The compass made it easier to travel a long way.

The compass

Sometimes people in different places have the same new idea. That is what happened with the compass. It was invented in China, Europe, and the Middle East. This happened at about the same time.

1100

Compass is first used to find direction in China.

◀ **1100–1150** ▶

Traders travel between Europe and Asia.

1075   1125   1150

Traveling and Trading

For years European traders traveled to Asia and back. They took gold, glass, and horses to trade. People in Asia did not have these things. The Europeans traded them for Asian goods. They traded for goods such as silk and spices.

Marco Polo lived in what is now Italy. In 1271 he left home to go to China. Polo traveled over land and ocean. His trip lasted for 25 years.

Marco Polo wrote a book about his trip. Many people read his book. Some wanted to travel like Polo. More and more people wanted maps.

◄ Hundreds of years ago, tools such as these astrolabes were used to make maps. Astrolabes showed travelers the position of the stars.

1190

Compass is first used in Europe and the Middle East.

1175   1200

▼ European traders traveled to find goods they could not buy at home. In Asia, they found spices, silk, and other goods.

1271

Marco Polo leaves for China.

1296

Marco Polo returns to Venice.

1225   1250   1275   1300

Charting the Coasts

During the 1300s, most long trips were by ship. The ships stayed close to the coasts. Sailors made charts. The charts told about the land along the coasts. These charts were called **portolans**.

The first portolans only had words. Later they had drawings of land. Some even showed towns and cities on the coast. Portolans started to look more like maps.

Portolans gave sailing directions. They showed the distance between places. They even showed where there were dangerous rocks in the ocean. This helped sailors find the best way to travel.

In the winter it was too dangerous to travel by ship. It was hard to see the coast. But the **compass** changed things. Sailors used compasses to find north, south, west, and east. The sailors could make better charts. Now they could travel in the winter. They did not have to see the land. They could still tell where they were.

1300

Sailors begin to use portolans.

portolan chart used for traveling by ship

▼ *Portolans were made of thin sheets of animal skin. They were viewed from all sides. This portolan shows the coasts along the Mediterranean Sea. South is at the top of the map.*

13

1350   1375   1400

Changing Views of the World

In the 1400s, **explorers** like Christopher Columbus discovered new lands. The explorers told **cartographers** about these places. They put the new places on their maps.

Martin Waldseemüller was a German cartographer. He used information from Columbus. He also used information from Amerigo Vespucci. Vespucci was an Italian explorer.

Waldseemüller made a new map. It was the first map to show America. He named America for Amerigo Vespucci. Soon other mapmakers put America on their maps.

Printed maps

*Around 1450 there was a new invention. This was the **printing press**. It made mapmaking easier and faster. Before this time all maps were made by hand. Now a mapmaker could make one map. Then hundreds of copies could be printed.*

1450

Printing press is invented.

explorer   person who looks for new lands
printing press   machine that prints books and other writing

▼ Martin Waldeemuller used news from Columbus to make this map. It was made in 1507. It shows America as a large island.

North America

South America

1492
Columbus makes his first trip.

1507
America appears on a world map.

1475   1500   1550   1600

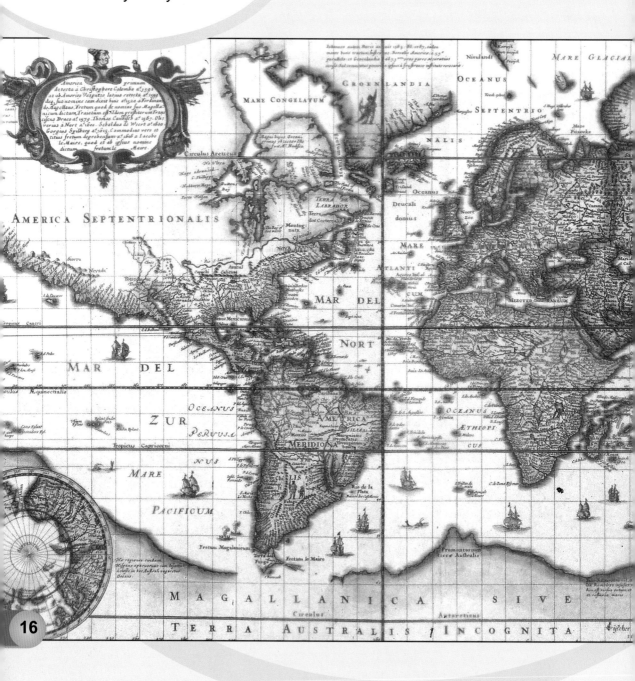

This map of 1635 used ▼ a new idea. Lands near the poles look larger than they really are.

atlas book of maps

1500

1525

Mercator's maps

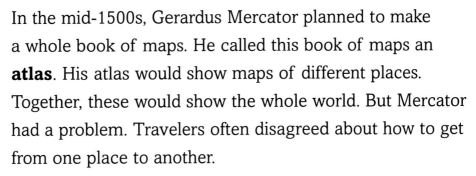

In the mid-1500s, Gerardus Mercator planned to make a whole book of maps. He called this book of maps an **atlas**. His atlas would show maps of different places. Together, these would show the whole world. But Mercator had a problem. Travelers often disagreed about how to get from one place to another.

Mercator knew why this happened. Travelers used a **compass**. A compass points in a straight line. But the Earth is curved. That makes it hard to figure out exactly where things are.

Mercator had a new idea. He changed his maps. He stretched out places near the North Pole and South Pole. They looked larger than they really are. Now straight lines on his maps stood for straight compass directions.

Many **cartographers** still use Mercator's ideas. Their maps are called Mercator Projections.

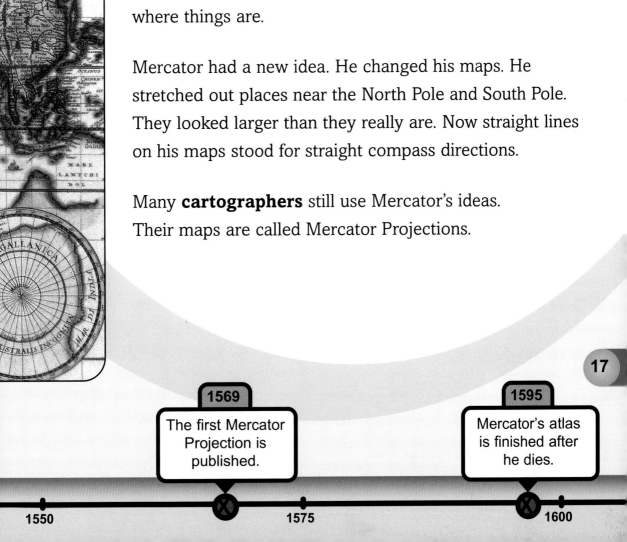

1569
The first Mercator Projection is published.

1595
Mercator's atlas is finished after he dies.

1550   1575   1600

New Mapmaking Tools

In the 1600s and 1700s, many European travelers explored the world. Some new inventions helped them.

The **sextant** was first used around 1757. It used the Sun to tell directions. It could tell how far north or south a ship was. Some older tools used the Sun, too. However, a sextant worked better.

Sailors began to use a new kind of **compass**. This compass was better at showing directions on long trips.

▼ *James Cook explored many islands. He explored the islands of Tahiti. This i a map of Tahiti made from Cook's trip.*

marine chronometer tool used to figure out time and location at sea
sextant tool that uses the Sun to find a location

But sailors still had trouble far out at sea. They needed to know the time to figure out where they were. In those days, watches were not exact enough. The **marine chronometer** solved the problem. It helped sailors figure out the time wherever they were.

All these new tools helped travelers. They brought back better information about places. This information helped **cartographers**. It helped them draw more exact maps.

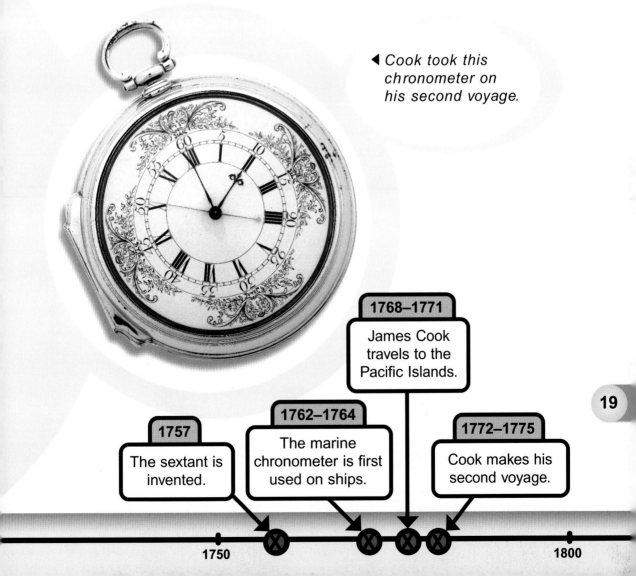

◀ *Cook took this chronometer on his second voyage.*

1768–1771
James Cook travels to the Pacific Islands.

1757
The sextant is invented.

1762–1764
The marine chronometer is first used on ships.

1772–1775
Cook makes his second voyage.

1750

1800

Up in the Air

In the 1700s and 1800s, there were more new inventions. They changed the way **cartographers** saw the world. One invention was the hot air balloon.

The higher you go, the more you can see of the Earth. Mapmakers could get a good view from a hilltop. They could go even higher in hot air balloons.

Another important invention was the camera. Now cartographers could study photographs. They could see exactly how an area of land looked.

Some mapmakers used these inventions together. People took photographs from high in the air. Mapmakers studied these **aerial photographs**. The photographs helped them make very exact maps of an area.

Camera tricks

One mapmaker wanted to get an aerial photo. He tied a camera to a kite. This did not work! Next he used a balloon. It carried a special camera. This time, his idea worked.

1783
The first hot air balloon flight takes place.

aerial photograph   photograph taken from overhead, in the air

1780

▼ This picture shows a hot air balloon flight. It happened in France in 1784.

1827

A French inventor takes the first photograph.

1858

The first aerial photograph is taken.

21

1800   1825   1850   1875

High-Tech Mapping

In the early 1900s, the airplane was invented. Airplanes helped change maps. Planes could fly much higher than hot air balloons. **Aerial photographs** could be taken from higher in the sky. These photographs showed larger areas of the Earth. They gave mapmakers more information to use.

Cartographers put aerial photographs together like a jigsaw. Each one showed part of the land. They studied the photographs. Then they drew maps to show what they saw.

But cartographers had some problems. Sometimes the airplanes tilted when taking photographs. Sometimes the airplanes flew higher for some photographs than for others. Sometimes the curve of Earth showed in a photograph. These things made it hard for the cartographers to make exact maps.

1903

First successful airplane flight takes place.

1900   1905   1910   1915

▼ *A photograph is not a map. Photographs show everything on a piece of land. A map only shows things the mapmaker decides to include.*

23

Computers and satellites

Aerial photographs made mapmaking much easier. But it still took a long time to make a map. First, someone had to draw each line by hand. Then, they had to color the maps by hand. Finally, the map had to be copied and printed.

In the 1970s **cartographers** started using computers to make maps. These maps are called **digital maps**. Computers can make maps that are very exact. Cartographers can store their maps on computers, too. That makes it easy to make changes later.

Satellites also have changed mapmaking. Satellites are machines that travel in space around Earth. Some satellites carry special cameras. They send the photographs back to computers on Earth. Then, cartographers use the photographs to make digital maps. Now, maps are more exact than ever before.

digital map   map made by a computer
satellite   object that travels in space around Earth

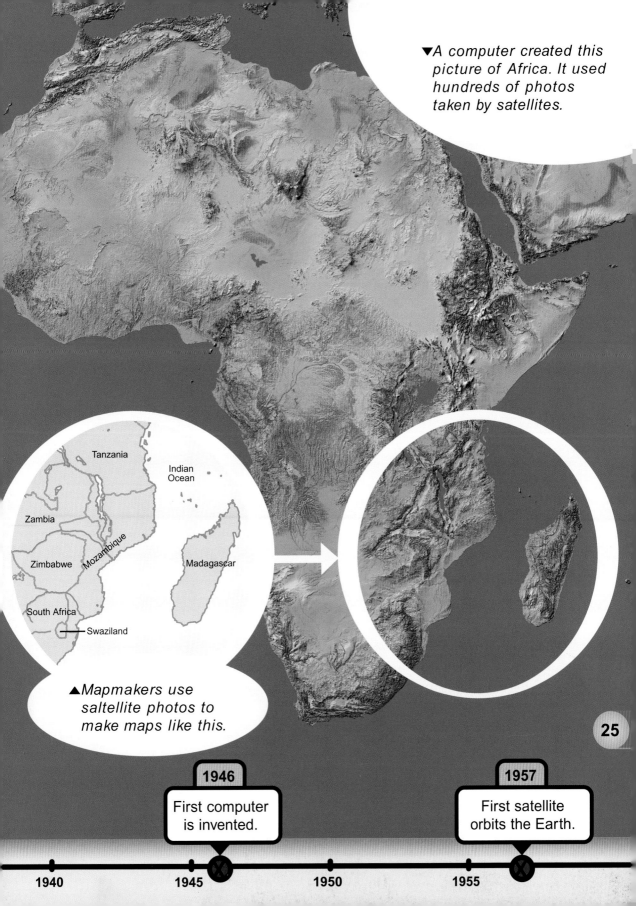

▼A computer created this picture of Africa. It used hundreds of photos taken by satellites.

Tanzania

Indian Ocean

Zambia

Zimbabwe

Mozambique

Madagascar

South Africa

Swaziland

▲Mapmakers use saltellite photos to make maps like this.

25

1946
First computer is invented.

1957
First satellite orbits the Earth.

1940   1945   1950   1955

Interactive maps

Today there are maps that work along with people. Many of these maps depend on **GPS**. GPS stands for **Global Positioning System**.

A GPS unit is a tiny computer. It uses signals from dozens of **satellites** high above Earth. The signals travel to GPS units on Earth. The GPS unit only needs four signals to tell where it is on Earth.

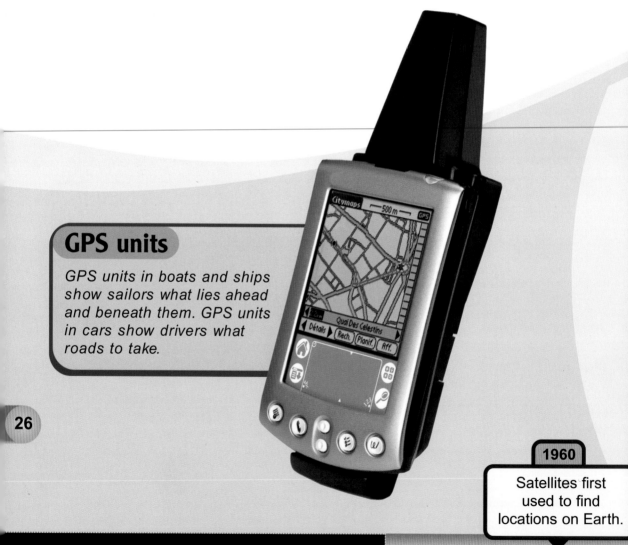

GPS units

GPS units in boats and ships show sailors what lies ahead and beneath them. GPS units in cars show drivers what roads to take.

1960

Satellites first used to find locations on Earth.

Global Positioning System (GPS) group of satellites that gives exact locations on Earth

You can also use a computer to get a map. You enter your starting place. Then, you enter where you want to go. In seconds the computer shows you a map. It also gives directions. It even tells you how many miles you have to travel.

▼ *This boy is using a computer to get directions to his friend's house.*

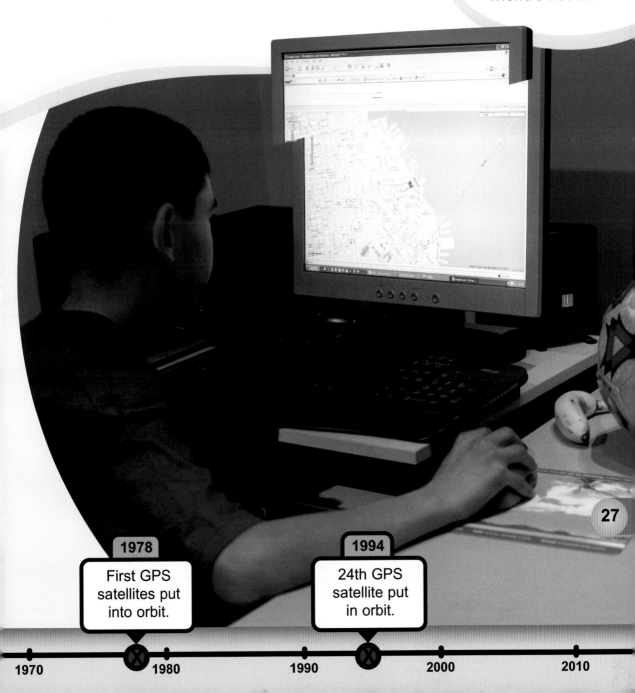

27

1978
First GPS satellites put into orbit.

1994
24th GPS satellite put in orbit.

1970   1980   1990   2000   2010

Then and Now

The work of **cartographers** has changed over the years. So have their maps. Study these two maps. Find Africa on the copy of Ptolemy's old map on this page. Now see how different Africa looks on the modern map on page 29! This is because parts of Africa were unknown in Ptolemy's time.

▼This map of the world was made in 1520.

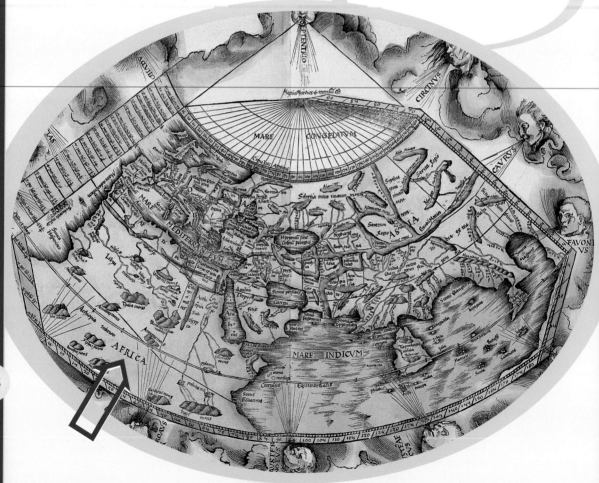

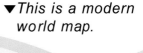
▼*This is a modern world map.*

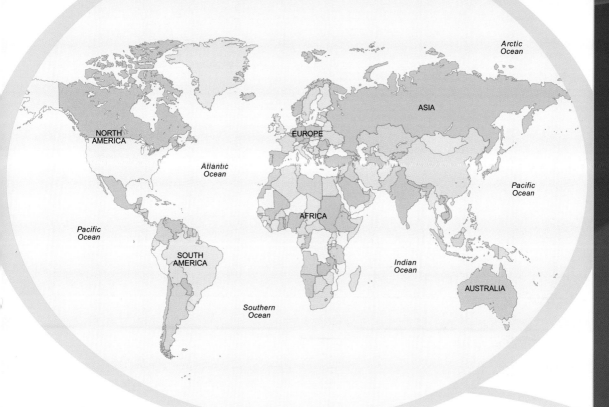

Mapmaking will keep changing. This is partly because Earth continues to change. Big storms can wash away areas of coast. The names and **borders** of countries can change. Cartographers must make new maps to show this information.

Glossary

aerial photograph photograph taken from overhead, in the air. Mapmakers use aerial photographs to study the land.

atlas book of maps. A world atlas has maps for each country in the world.

border imaginary line that separates land. The states of the United States are separated by borders.

cartographer person who makes maps. For many years, cartographers made maps by hand.

compass tool that tells directions. Hikers can use a compass to find their way.

digital map map made by a computer. Computers put information together to make digital maps.

explorer person who looks for new lands. Christopher Columbus was an explorer.

Global Positioning System (GPS) group of satellites that gives exact locations on Earth. Ships use the Global Positioning System to know where they are.

marine chronometer tool used to figure out time and location at sea. The marine chronometer helped sailors know where they were.

portolan chart used for traveling by ship. Sailors made portolans to help them find their way at sea.

printing press machine that prints books and other writing. Most newspapers are printed on a printing press.

satellite object that travels around Earth.

sextant tool that uses the Sun to find location. Hundreds of years ago, sailors used the sextant to find their way.

Want to Know More?

Books to read

- DiSpezio, Michael A. *Map Mania: Discovering Where You Are and Getting to Where You Aren't.* New York: Sterling, 2003.

- Olesky, Walter. *Mapping the Seas.* New York: Franklin Watts, 2003.

- Olesky, Walter. *Maps in History.* New York: Franklin Watts, 2002.

- Romano Young, Karen. *Small Worlds: Maps and Mapmaking.* New York: Scholastic, 2002.

DVDs

- *Using Maps and Globes* (Educational Video Network, Inc., 2004). A guide to maps and globes and how they help us understand the world.

Websites

- http://www.nationalgeographic.com/maps
  Learn more about maps and how to make them.

- http://www.mapquest.com
  A site where you can print out a map that shows you how to get from one place to another.

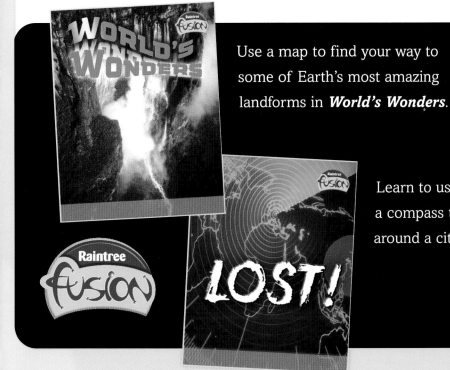

Use a map to find your way to some of Earth's most amazing landforms in **World's Wonders**.

Learn to use just a map and a compass to find your way around a city in **Lost!**

Index

aerial photographs 20, 21, 22, 23, 24, 25

Africa 25, 28, 29

airplanes 22

America 14, 15

astrolabes 10

atlas 16, 17

borders 4, 5, 29

cameras 20, 24

charts 12

clay maps 7

Columbus, Christopher 14, 15

compasses 8, 9, 10, 12, 17, 18

computers 24, 25, 26, 27

Cook, James 18, 19

digital maps 24

earliest maps 6–7

explorers 14, 18

GPS (Global Positioning System) 26–27

hand-drawn maps 6, 14

hot air balloons 20, 21

interactive maps 26–27

inventions 9, 18, 19, 20

mapmakers (cartographers) 5, 6, 14, 17, 20, 22, 23, 24, 28, 29

marine chronometers 19

Mercator, Gerardus 17

Mercator Projections 17

North and South Poles 9, 16, 17

Polo, Marco 10, 11

portolans 12, 13

printing press 14

Ptolemy 6, 7, 28

sailors 12, 18, 19, 26

satellites 24, 25, 26, 27

sextants 18, 19

Tahiti 18

trade routes 8

traders 9, 10, 11

travelers 5, 8–9, 10, 17, 18, 19

Vespucci, Amerigo 14

Waldseemüller, Martin 14, 15